NOW YOU CAN READ....

The Three Billy-Goats Gruff

STORY ADAPTED BY LUCY KINCAID

ILLUSTRATED BY CLIVE SPONG

BRIMAX BOOKS • CAMBRIDGE • ENGLAND

It had been a long winter with
lots of snow. Food had been hard
to find and the Three Billy-goats
Gruff were very thin. But now the
snow had gone from the pasture
and the grass was looking fresh
and green.

"I shall go to the top pasture today," said First Billy-goat Gruff, who was also the smallest. "The grass is always much greener and sweeter up there."

"Take care the troll does not catch you," said his brothers who were playing at pushing with their horns. "We will follow you later."

To get to the top pasture the three Billy-goats Gruff had to cross a stream. The water was deep and cold and the only way over it was by the humpy-backed bridge.

Underneath the bridge, in the dark and the damp, lived a bad-tempered troll. He had eyes as big as saucers and a nose as long and as sharp as a poker. Everyone was afraid of him, and there was nothing he liked better than eating goat for dinner.

The troll was splashing his feet in the stream and trying to catch a fish with his toes when he heard, tip...tap...tip...tap... above his head.

"Who is that walking over MY bridge?" he shouted.

"It is I," called First Billy-goat
Gruff, trembling like a leaf.
"Then I will have you for my
dinner," roared the troll.
"Please don't do that," pleaded
First Billy-goat Gruff. "I am
very small and thin. One mouthful
and I would be gone. My brother
is much fatter than I."

"Then I will wait, and have HIM for my dinner instead of you," said the troll. "Be on your way before I change my mind."

First Billy-goat Gruff did not need telling twice. He skipped off to the pasture as fast as his legs would take him.

The bad-tempered troll went back under the bridge and teased the toads while he waited for his dinner to come. Presently, he heard more footsteps tapping across the bridge . . . tip . . . tap . . . tip . . . tap "Who is that walking over MY bridge?" he shouted.

"It is I," called Second Billy-goat Gruff.

"Then I will have you for my dinner," roared the troll.

"Please don't do that," pleaded Second Billy-goat Gruff. "It has been a long hard winter. I am still very bony and thin. My brother will be coming this way soon, he is much fatter than I."

"Then I will wait and have HIM
for my dinner instead of you,"
said the troll. "Be on your way
before I change my mind."
Second Billy-goat Gruff did not
need to be told twice either,
and quickly joined First Billy-goat
Gruff in the top pasture.

The troll sat under the bridge in the damp and the dark and waited. He was getting very hungry and more and more bad-tempered. He tried to catch a fish but couldn't. And he couldn't tease the toads because they had hidden.

He waited and waited. He waited
a very long time, but at last,
he heard footsteps above his head.
Tip ... tap ... tip ... tap ... tip ... tap
"Who is that walking over MY
bridge?" he shouted.

"It is I!" called Third Billy-goat Gruff.

"Then I am coming to eat you!" roared the troll.
"Come and try!" shouted Third Billy-goat Gruff.

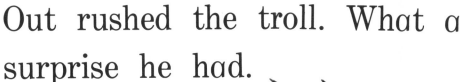

Out rushed the troll. What a surprise he had.

The Third Billy-goat Gruff was
also the largest Billy-goat Gruff.
He had long curly horns on his
head, and a beard hanging from
his chin. He was afraid of
no one.

He caught the troll with his
horns and tossed him up into the
air. Up...up...up went the troll.
And then, down...down...down
came the troll.

Third Billy-goat Gruff tossed him again. He tossed him so high he almost reached the moon.

Then while the troll was tumbling through the sky, Third Billy-goat Gruff went to the top pasture and joined his brothers.
The troll NEVER came back and from that day onwards it was quite safe to cross the humpy-backed bridge.

All these appear in the pages of
the story. Can you find them?

Second Billy-goat Gruff

First Billy-goat Gruff

troll

Third Billy-goat Gruff